FEEDING YOURSELF

VICKI COBB
Pictures by Marylin Hafner

J. B. Lippincott   New York

Library of Congress Cataloging-in-Publication Data
Cobb, Vicki.
    Feeding yourself / by Vicki Cobb ; illustrated by Marylin Hafner — 1st ed.
        p.   cm.
    Summary: Describes how knives, forks, spoons, and chopsticks came
to be invented and how they are used today in eating.
    ISBN 0-397-32324-7 : $.   ISBN 0-397-32325-5 (lib. bdg.) : $
    1. Flatware—History—Juvenile literature. [1. Flatware.]   I. Hafner,
Marylin, ill.   II. Title.
GT2948.C63   1989   88-14192
394.1'2'09—dc19   CIP
                                                           AC

Time for dinner. What are you having? Maybe it's soup, or steak and mashed potatoes, or stir-fried vegetables. Suppose you didn't have a knife, fork, pair of chopsticks, or a spoon.

In some parts of the world it's polite to eat with your fingers all the time. But for preparing meals and eating many kinds of dishes, tools are useful inventions.

People did not always use eating tools. About five hundred years ago, food was put out on platters in the middle of the table. Each person used a large, hard cracker called a *trencher* as a plate. Gravy made the trenchers soggy, so extra trenchers were put on the table. People took food from the platters with their fingers and put it on their trenchers.

No one knows who invented the knife, fork, chopsticks, or spoon. But they have been used to prepare food and to get it to your mouth for centuries. Here are their stories.

THE KNIFE

Thousands of years ago, people lived in caves. When a caveman wanted to crack open a nut, he smashed it with a rock. The rock became a kind of hammer. Then someone must have discovered that if the hammer had a sharp edge, it could cut wood. And so the ax was invented.

A small stone with a sharp edge could be used to cut things that were softer than wood. Such a small, sharp stone became the first knife.

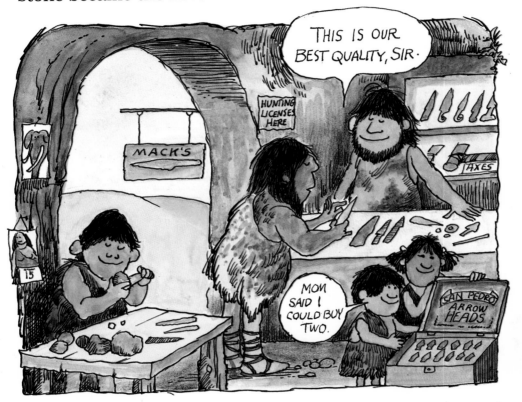

Cavemen figured out which were the best kinds of stones for making knives and all sorts of cutting tools. Cavemen made so many different kinds of tools from rocks that we call the time they lived in the Stone Age.

Thousands of years later, people discovered how to make metals such as bronze and iron. Metal was stronger than stone and could be made into many more shapes. Knives began to look more like the knives we use now.

Soon everyone carried a knife. It was the all-purpose eating tool.

People began setting the table with a knife for each person about two hundred years ago. A table knife is used in several ways:

A knife gets food in shape for your mouth.

THE FORK

The first fork was probably a pointed stick. You've used the earliest kind of fork if you've ever roasted a marshmallow over a campfire. You also know that it has its problems.

Why not make a tool with more than one point? With two points there is a better chance of holding speared food. A fork that had two points, or prongs, was invented by the ancient Romans. They used their two-pronged fork for cooking. The word *fork* has come to mean "divide into two or more branches."

Although people have used forks for cooking for thousands of years, they have only been eating with them for the last two centuries.

About five hundred years ago, some kings and queens put forks on their tables. But people who first used a fork at dinner were thought to be very strange.

A two-pronged fork is only good for spearing food. Today's table fork has four prongs. The four prongs close together keep food from slipping between the cracks. So you can use a table fork to scoop up food, like a spoon.

A fork and knife together make a great team for cutting
meat. If you're right-handed, you stab the meat and hold it
still with the fork in your left hand and saw away with the
knife in your right.

In most countries of the world, people lift the meat to the mouth with their left hand as soon as it is cut. But Americans put down the knife and then move the fork to their right hand before lifting the food to their mouth.

CONFUSING ISN'T IT?

CHOPSTICKS

There's only one easy way to pick up a pea with your fingers. You use your thumb and your index finger like pincers. The pea can be neatly lifted to your mouth. Now suppose you want to pick up a pea without touching it with your fingers. Thousands of years ago, the Chinese invented just the tool to do this: chopsticks.

Chopsticks are simply two slim sticks about as long as a man's hand. Chinese chopsticks have blunt ends. Japanese chopsticks are slimmer and have pointed ends.

CHINESE

JAPANESE

I WONDER IF I COULD LEARN TO USE THOSE.

Millions of Asian people use chopsticks instead of knives and forks. Chinese and Japanese children all learn how, just as Western children learn to use a knife and fork.

Everyone can learn to use chopsticks. If you don't have chopsticks handy, you can practice with two pencils.

TAKE ONE CHOPSTICK OR PENCIL AND LAY THE NARROW, POINTED END ACROSS THE LAST JOINT OF YOUR 4th FINGER.

REST THE WIDE END IN THE HOLLOW WHERE YOUR THUMB MEETS YOUR HAND. YOUR THUMB HOLDS THE CHOPSTICK IN PLACE SO THAT IT DOESN'T MOVE. THIS CHOPSTICK SHOULD BE HELD FIRMLY IN PLACE.

2.

3.

4.

1.

5.

WIDE END

NARROW POINTED END

THE SECOND CHOPSTICK IS THE ONE THAT MOVES & DOES ALL THE WORK PICKING UP FOOD. HOLD IT AS YOU HOLD A PENCIL WHEN YOU WRITE, WITH THE TIP OF YOUR THUMB & YOUR INDEX FINGER, LETTING IT REST ON YOUR MIDDLE FINGER.

MOVE THIS CHOPSTICK OUT & IN, SO THE ENDS OF BOTH CHOPSTICKS CAN COME TOGETHER LIKE TWEEZERS.

LOOKS SIMPLE ENOUGH!

21

Practice picking up small objects, and pretty soon you will become comfortable using your chopsticks. From time to time, you may have to tap the ends of both chopsticks to keep them even.

Most Asian food is already cut into small pieces when it's brought to the table, so knives are not needed.

23

Chinese restaurants will give you chopsticks if you ask. It feels right to eat Chinese and Japanese food with chopsticks, not forks.

Chopstick experts can eat very quickly.

The word *chopsticks* means "fast sticks."

THE SPOON

Imagine trying to drink from a stream. You cup your hands and use them as a bowl to carry the water to your mouth.

People need bowls to carry liquids. A knife or fork or chopsticks simply won't do.

The first bowl users put a small bowl at the end of a handle. This tool could dish up liquids by the mouthful. It could stir soups and scoop up a small bit for tasting.

IT SMELLS GOOD!

The spoon is one of the earliest tools ever invented. It is used all over the world.

Spoons come in different sizes and shapes to do different jobs.

ICE CREAM SODA SPOON

LADLE

TEASPOON

MEASURING SPOONS

TABLESPOON

WOODEN SPOON

KITCHEN SPOONS

GRAPEFRUIT SPOON
WITH SERRATED TIP

SLOTTED SPOON

SERVING SPOON

SOUP SPOON

31

Eating tools are perfect for the jobs they have to do. How clever people were to invent them!